OLIVER CROMWELL AND THE CIVIL WAR

Stephen White-Thomson

Illustrations by Gerry Wood

D1336966

LIFE AND TIMES

First published in 1984 by
Wayland (Publishers) Ltd,
49 Lansdowne Place, Hove,
East Sussex BN3 1HF, England

© Copyright 1984 Wayland (Publishers) Ltd

ISBN 0 85078 458 1

Phototypeset by Planagraphic Typesetters Ltd
Printed in Italy by G. Canale & C.S.p.A., Turin
Bound in the U.K. by The Pitman Press, Bath

Contents

1 THE STORY OF OLIVER CROMWELL

Early life

Oliver Cromwell 1599-1658.

Oliver Cromwell's signature. The 'P' stands for Protector.

The middle years of the seventeenth century were a time of great upheaval in Britain. In 1642, Civil War broke out. There followed many years of violent warfare, when the English, Scots and Irish fought their fellow country-men, brother against brother and father against son.

The Civil War blew up out of a power struggle between King Charles I, and Parliament. One of the leading supporters of Parliament was a man called Oliver Cromwell. Although he became the most powerful man in England, he had a humble start to his life.

Oliver Cromwell was born in Huntingdon in 1599. His family farmed cattle and corn, and were well known in the district of East Anglia. The Cromwells had been friends with King James I, who reigned from 1603 to 1625, and the king had stayed three nights on the farm with Oliver's uncle on his way to claim the English throne. Oliver himself had no great love for royalty and, less than fifty years after that royal visit, he sent Charles I, King of England, to his death.

Oliver Cromwell was a large, strong man with plain tastes and simple pleasures. He married Elizabeth Bourchier in 1620 and spent the next few years raising a family and farming. He became known as 'Lord of the Fens' because he stood up for the interests of ordinary people when they were threatened by rich merchants or landowners.

During this time, he began to believe that he had been chosen by God to perform an important task on earth. He had no idea what this would be and he had few ambitions apart from working hard and living a godly life. The outbreak of the Civil War changed all that.

The young Oliver greets a worker on his Fenland farm.

The soldier

In the Civil War, Oliver Cromwell proved to be a brave soldier and an excellent commander. His military talents were soon realized and, during the course of the war, he was promoted from cavalry officer to the Commander-in-Chief of the parliamentary forces. When war became certain in 1642, it was natural that Cromwell should fight for Parliament because he was angered by Charles I's behaviour and policies during the 1630s.

Cromwell took only a small part in the early stages of the war. He raised a small troop of cavalry in Huntingdonshire but missed the first major battle between the two sides at Edgehill. In 1643, he brooded on the reasons why

Parliament was failing to win. He realized that Parliament's soldiers were inferior to the king's troops. They were not so brave or dashing. He needed 'men of spirit', so he started to raise a force of 'godly men' in East Anglia. These men, nicknamed the 'Ironsides', became the best soldiers of the war.

In 1645, the 'Ironsides' became the backbone of a disciplined and professional 'New Model Army'. Under Cromwell's stern leadership this tough army spearheaded Parliament's victories at Naseby, Dunbar, and Worcester. The Royalists lost the war. Parliament, and Cromwell, were triumphant.

Cromwell was always confident that he would win because he believed that God was on his side. Certainly, God seemed to favour him. He never lost a battle in the field. However, he had another battle which was not so easy to win. The men who had opposed the king split into two different camps: the soldiers of the army against the Members of Parliament (M.P.s) and their supporters. It was not as a soldier, but as a politician that Cromwell had to try and sort out this enormous problem.

A Roundhead cavalryman.

Left *Cromwell recruits men in East Anglia for his crack force of 'Ironsides'.*

The politician

Before the Civil War, Cromwell's experience as a politician had been very limited. His political skills were to be sorely tested in the years following Parliament's victory.

Victory in war often creates more problems than defeat. The Parliamentary side had won and the victors now believed that they could run the country in the way they wanted. Unfortunately, the soldiers had different ideas to the men who sat in Parliament about how this should happen. Cromwell was in the unique position of being both a soldier and an M.P., so he was powerfully placed to influence the future of his country.

Cromwell began by supporting the soldiers in the struggle between the army and Parliament. In 1648, with Cromwell's approval, Colonel Pride marched into Parliament and threw out the M.P.s who were against the army. The remaining M.P.s — only a handful of them — were called the 'Rump' Parliament. They sat until 1653. During that time, and under pressure from Cromwell, they brought the king to the trial that led to his execution and the setting-up of the Commonwealth.

Cromwell discovered that England without a king behaved like a chicken without its head, which rushes around uncontrollably in all directions. After he had angrily dismissed the Rump Parliament, Cromwell experimented with new Parliaments, but dissolved them because the members spent all their time arguing. He realized that the country needed one man in control to fill the vacuum left after Charles I's death. Although he refused the title of king, he became the Lord Protector in 1653 and governed the country with the help of the major-generals — his army commanders — until his death in 1658.

A meeting of Parliament in 1642.

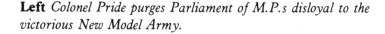

Left *Colonel Pride purges Parliament of M.P.s disloyal to the victorious New Model Army.*

His achievements

Cromwell once gave some advice to a man who was painting his portrait. He wanted to be painted as he really was, 'warts and all'. He hoped that the portrait would be truthful, showing the good as well as the bad. He knew that he was far from perfect and had not achieved all that he had set out to do. Nevertheless, his achievements were considerable. Even Clarendon, a famous Royalist historian, was forced to admit that, 'all things seemed to succeed at home and abroad to his wish'.

Cromwell's success as a military commander in the Civil War was one of the main reasons for Parliament's victory over the king. Whether or not you think that was an achievement depends on which side you support, but no one can deny that he was a brilliant soldier.

After the Restoration in 1660 Cromwell's head was dug up and his head displayed before a hostile crowd.

This statue of Cromwell outside the Houses of Parliament reflects the importance of his role in British History.

After the war, Cromwell found that the game of politics had different rules to the battlefield. There could be no decisive attacks because there was no clear-cut enemy. As Lord Protector, he became very frustrated because Parliaments tried to ignore his ambitious plans for reform.

Nevertheless, he did bring peace to the country after the years of bloody war. During his time in power, trade prospered, the navy became strong once more, and people could hold their religious beliefs without any fear of prosecution.

In 1660, two years after Oliver's death and the failure of his son Richard to carry on his work, Charles II was restored to the throne. Public opinion swung violently away from Cromwell. His body was dug up and hanged at Tyburn. This was the people's harsh verdict on Cromwell, but looking back over the years, he seems a talented man whose remarkable personality dominated some of the most turbulent years of British history.

2 THE BUILD-UP OF TENSION

Money

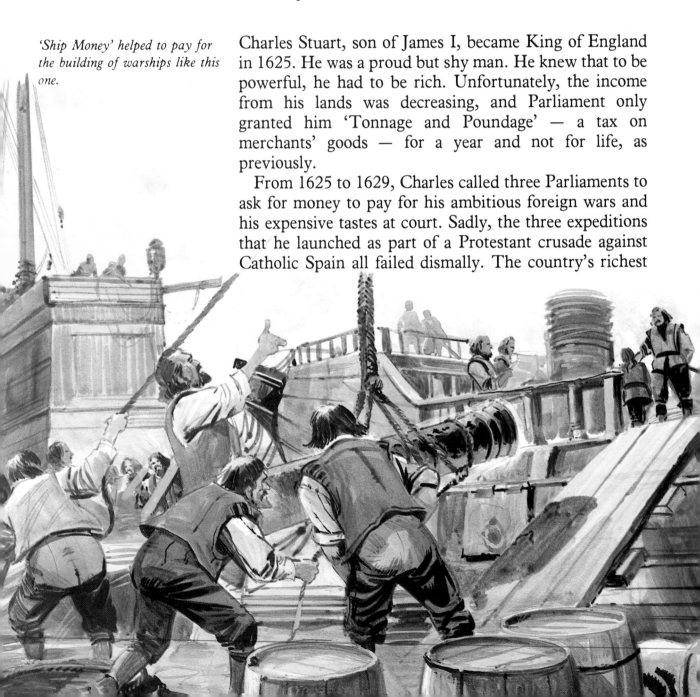

'Ship Money' helped to pay for the building of warships like this one.

Charles Stuart, son of James I, became King of England in 1625. He was a proud but shy man. He knew that to be powerful, he had to be rich. Unfortunately, the income from his lands was decreasing, and Parliament only granted him 'Tonnage and Poundage' — a tax on merchants' goods — for a year and not for life, as previously.

From 1625 to 1629, Charles called three Parliaments to ask for money to pay for his ambitious foreign wars and his expensive tastes at court. Sadly, the three expeditions that he launched as part of a Protestant crusade against Catholic Spain all failed dismally. The country's richest and most influential men who sat in Parliament were not prepared to pay for failure.

The idea was growing among M.P.s that Parliament should control the royal purse-strings and that the king should not be allowed to raise taxes without their consent. This feeling was expressed in a 'Petition of Right' in 1628, to which Charles reluctantly agreed.

A year later, Charles was so angry with Parliament that he sent his troops to put an end to its sitting. For the next eleven years, from 1629 to 1640, he ruled without Parliament.

Charles now had to find money from other sources. He forced people to loan him money and fined anyone who did not attend church. Most notorious of all, he raised 'Ship Money'. This was supposed to be a tax on coastal towns to pay for warships but Charles extended it inland and used it for his own purposes. Cromwell's cousin, John Hampden, refused to pay. Although he lost a famous court case, it turned him into a popular hero; five out of the twelve judges declared the tax illegal.

The trouble was that Charles tried to raise money from the class of people who were in a position to complain the loudest. These complaints were voiced in Parliament. By not learning to work *with* Parliament, Charles created a rod for his own back.

John Hampden, a leading Parliamentarian and a cousin of Cromwell.

Right *John Hampden before his judges in court having refused to pay 'Ship Money'.*

Religion

A Puritan about to have his ears cut off for disagreeing with Charles I about religion.

Charles I was a very religious man. He was head of the Church of England and wanted all his people to share the same religious beliefs.

Unfortunately, this did not happen. The tumultuous events of the Reformation in the sixteenth century had smashed the unity of the Catholic Church. People still believed in the Christian God, but they worshipped Him in very different ways. Most Englishmen had become Protestants — but there were many different types of Protestants. The only thing that united them was a fear of Catholics. Some of them thought that the English Church needed to be changed. Cromwell was one of these men.

Sadly, Charles was out of step with the thinking of his time. He made a serious mistake in appointing William Laud as his Archbishop of Canterbury. Laud was a 'little, low, red-faced man,' with a fiery temper.

14

Laud made the mistake of persecuting Puritans. In 1637, three Puritans — Prynne, Bastwick and Burton — had their ears cut off for holding the popular belief that there should be no bishops. Apart from this brutality, for which he was despised, Laud was suspected of trying to return the country to Catholicism. There were angry riots in Scotland when he made them use the English Prayer Book which led to war between the two countries.

Laud became increasingly unpopular with certain powerful sections of society. So did the king and his Catholic wife, Henrietta Maria, who both sympathized with Laud's reforms. In 1640, Laud was imprisoned by order of Parliament, but not before great damage had been done to Charles's cause. A year later, the king's opponents in Parliament reversed Laud's reforms and abolished bishops in the Church of England. The king had meddled with people's religious beliefs — and was to pay the penalty.

William Laud, Archbishop of Canterbury 1633-40.

King or Parliament?

The build-up to the Civil War was a struggle for power between king and Parliament. Charles I believed in the Divine Right of Kings. This meant that he saw himself as chosen by God. He therefore had absolute power over his subjects and could do whatever he wanted.

However, there was a group of powerful men in Parliament who believed that Charles was not perfect. If his policies went against the 'ancient liberties' of the kingdom which Parliament had to protect, he could be disobeyed.

The tense situation might never have led to war if Charles had been a better leader but, as Archbishop Laud once said, 'the king neither is, nor knows how to be, great'. People will forgive their king almost anything if he

Below King Charles I in happier days takes a boat down the River Thames with his family.

16

is successful. Unfortunately, everything Charles was involved in turned out to be a disaster. His subjects saw their wealth and their religion threatened, and had to respond to safeguard their interests.

Parliament got at Charles by criticizing his advisers. The king had three close friends who wanted to boost the royal power which is why they were so hated by Parliament. They were the dashing Duke of Buckingham; Archbishop Laud; and the haughty Earl of Strafford, known as 'Black Tom'. They all met with gruesome ends — Buckingham was assassinated in 1628, and Strafford and Laud were both executed by order of Parliament in the 1640s.

Charles had been humiliated by his enemies in Parliament, and forced to sacrifice his most faithful supporters. However, some people thought that Parliament had gone too far. They started to rally round the king, who prepared his revenge. The country tottered on the brink of war.

Charles I's seal.

Below left *Queen Henrietta Maria.*

Below right *King Charles I.*

King Charles I enters Parliament and discovers that his enemies have escaped.

18

3 THE OUTBREAK OF WAR

The flashpoint

On 3rd January 1642, Charles entered Parliament with a troop of heavily-armed soldiers in support. He had come to arrest the five Members of Parliament who were causing him so much trouble — John Pym, John Hampden, Denzil Holles, William Strode, and Arthur Haselrig. Typically, he had dithered. His plans had become well known and the five members had plenty of time to escape into the safety of London's backstreets. In the House of Commons, Charles saw that his enemies were no longer there. He said in disgust, 'I see all my birds have flown'.

Charles made a great mistake in using a show of armed force at such a delicate time. However, he had been greatly provoked by the activities of his enemies during the 'Short' and 'Long' Parliaments that met in 1640.

Charles's opponents, led by John Pym, were desperate to reduce the king's power. They refused to grant him money to fight the Scots who were invading England, or put down a rebellion in Ireland, until they got what they wanted — the parliamentary right to control the army, reform the Church, and appoint the king's ministers.

Charles could not sit by and watch his power drain away. Many people thought that Pym had gone too far. They switched over to the king's side because they preferred to be governed by the king — even if he did make mistakes — than by Pym and the Puritans.

After the failure of the arrest of the five members, war seemed unavoidable. Charles left London, raised his standard at Nottingham on 22nd August 1642, and issued a call to arms. People now had to decide who to fight for. The Civil War had begun.

John Pym, leader of the opposition to Charles I in Parliament.

Prince Rupert raises the royal standard at Nottingham in 1642.

Above *Battle of Edgehill.*

A musketeer.

The country takes sides

Most people did not want war and did not know who to fight for. As Sir Arthur Haselrig said despairingly, 'the people care not what government they live under so long as they may plough and go to market'. The war was about whether the king or Parliament should take the lead in governing the country. Plenty of people were prepared to argue about it, but when it came to risking their lives for one side or the other, that was different.

Nevertheless, two sides did slowly emerge. The group that supported Parliament were called 'Roundheads' because of the cropped hair of the London apprentices who fought for them. They included merchants; Puritans; the majority of Londoners; the navy; and, after January 1644, the Scots. The king's supporters were known as 'Cavaliers' after the Spanish soldiers called *Cavalieros.*

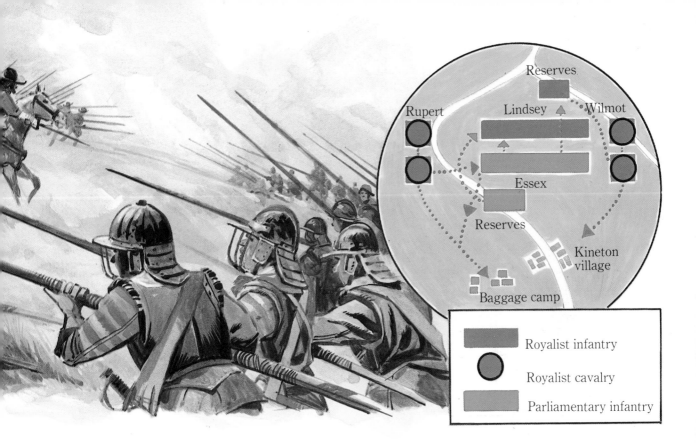

They included many great landowners; conservative people who lived in the north and west of the kingdom; and Members of Parliament who disagreed with Pym. But the sides were not always clear-cut and quite often members of the same family fought on different sides.

The first battle was fought on 23rd October 1642 at Edgehill. Neither side won but blood had been spilled. Anyone who witnessed the ferocity of the fighting knew that this would not be a short war as everyone had hoped, but would drag on for many years.

After the battle, Charles delayed and lost a good chance to shorten the war by failing to chase the parliamentary army back into London. He chose instead a slow-moving, three-pronged attack on the capital which was repulsed at the Battle of Turnham Green. He retreated to Oxford. He set up his court there and, as his Cavaliers drank and made merry, Charles tried to work out a plan for the victory that would give him back his lost authority.

A pikeman.

4 CIVIL WAR

The armies

The armies that fought in the Civil War were tiny compared with modern standards. They were made up of cavalry divisions — men on horseback — who spearheaded the attacks with wild and terrifying charges, and the 'poor foot', the pikemen and musketeers of the infantry regiments, that made up the bulk of the armies. There were few volunteers. Most were conscripts who had been bullied into joining one side or the other. The soldiers were often unwilling to fight outside their own counties and men deserted in their hundreds.

Both sides had difficulties raising money to keep their armies in the field. However, Parliament with its grip on

London and the major ports, was better off than the king who was forced to sell the Crown Jewels to survive.

In the early days, the troops were seldom paid, so they plundered the countryside and towns they passed through to make up for it. Keeping discipline was a great problem to all the commanders. The finest fighting force before 1644 was the Royalist cavalry, led by the swashbuckling Prince Rupert, nephew of the king. They were magnificently brave and spirited men, but their lack of discipline was disastrous for the Royalist cause.

It was Cromwell who first realized the importance of putting together a 'professional' army, one that was properly trained, decently paid and strictly disciplined. An army to be led by soldiers and not politicians such as the Earl of Manchester, whose leadership was weakened by the fear that, 'if we beat the king ninety-nine times, yet he is king still.'

In 1645, the New Model Army was formed. It was a professional force of 14,000 infantry and 7,000 cavalry led by Sir Thomas Fairfax, with Cromwell as second in command. This army tipped the military balance in Parliament's favour and swiftly led to Charles's defeat.

Royalist soldiers (on the left) and Parliamentary soldiers (on the right).

Marston Moor

The Earl of Essex, a leading Parliamentary general.

In the early months of 1644, the situation looked good for King Charles. His plan was to crush London in a pincer movement from the north and west. The scheme met with disaster on 2nd July 1644 at the Battle of Marston Moor, a few miles west of York.

The Royalists, led by Prince Rupert and the Earl of Newcastle, were beseiged in York by an army of soldiers from the Earl of Manchester's Eastern Association, the Scottish army, and Sir Thomas Fairfax's 'Northerners'. Prince Rupert, as yet unbeaten, and followed everywhere by his pet poodle, 'Boy', (who he had jokingly promoted to major-general), broke out of York. The two forces came face to face on Marston Moor and drew up in battle order.

The foot soldiers stood in the centre, a bristling hedgehog of pikes, with the musketeers stationed in the gaps. To their left and right, the cavalry waited for the order to charge. The Cavaliers played dice, the Roundheads knelt and prayed. The sun beat down all day until the late afternoon when a summer thunderstorm struck. Just as the Royalists were breaking rank to eat, thinking that there would be no battle that day, the Roundheads attacked.

On one wing, Cromwell's 'Ironsides' drove back the Royalist cavalry but Manchester's infantry was checked by the Earl of Newcastle's famous white-coated Northumbrians, who also destroyed Fairfax's cavalry on the other wing.

As the bells were ringing to celebrate a Royalist victory, Cromwell's 'Ironsides' charged again and routed the Royalists. It turned into a massacre. Cromwell's prayers had been answered: 'God made them as stubble to our swords' he wrote after the battle. It was a disaster for Charles, but he was not completely beaten yet.

Sir Thomas Fairfax, commander-in-chief of the New Model Army.

Opposite A map of the important battles and other sites of the Civil War.

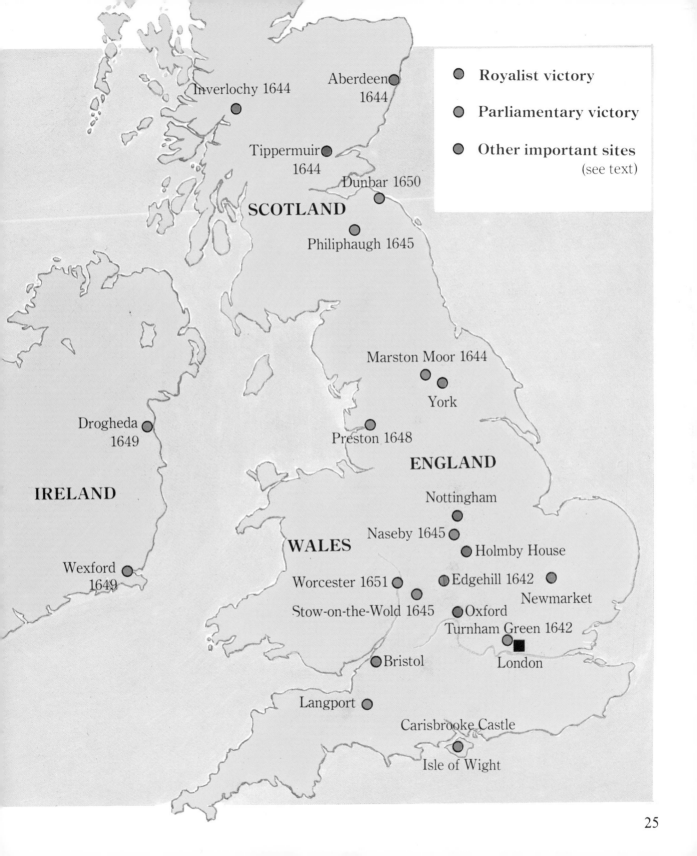

Inverlochy 1644

Aberdeen 1644

Tippermuir 1644

Dunbar 1650

SCOTLAND

Philiphaugh 1645

Royalist victory

Parliamentary victory

Other important sites
(see text)

IRELAND

Drogheda 1649

Wexford 1649

Marston Moor 1644

York

Preston 1648

ENGLAND

Nottingham

Naseby 1645

Holmby House

WALES

Worcester 1651

Edgehill 1642

Newmarket

Stow-on-the-Wold 1645

Oxford

Turnham Green 1642

Bristol

London

Langport

Carisbrooke Castle

Isle of Wight

25

Montrose and his Highlanders

Scotland did not play an honourable part in the war. She joined whichever side paid the most or seemed the most likely to introduce the Scottish brand of Protestantism into England. The Scots started the war fighting against the king and ended up fighting for the king's son.

In the bloodiest years of the Civil War, however, the Scots fought on Parliament's side. They played an important part in Charles's defeat at Marston Moor (see page 24). After that disaster, Charles had to grasp at straws to survive. He knew that many of the Highland Scots were Royalists at heart. So he sent James Graham, the Earl of Montrose, on a desperate mission into the rugged mountains of Scotland to raise a Royalist army.

Against all the odds, Montrose won a series of astonishing victories against his arch enemy, the Marquis of Argyll, who supported Parliament. He gathered together a small force of fierce Highlanders. They were joined by 1,600 ferocious warriors from Ireland, led by the fearless giant, Alasdair Macdonald.

On 1st September 1644, Montrose's ill-equipped and outnumbered army routed their enemies at the Battle of Tippermuir. The victorious army went on the rampage, sacking Aberdeen and massacring the Campbell clan at the Battle of Inverlochy, fought in the freezing conditions of a Scottish winter.

Montrose brought his army south to support his king, but he was betrayed. His troops were cut to pieces at the Battle of Philiphaugh in September 1645. Hundreds of the camp followers, women and children, were mercilessly thrown into a nearby river and drowned. Miraculously, Montrose escaped and fled to Norway. The Scottish gamble had failed. Time was running out for Charles I.

Opposite *Montrose's wild Highlanders attack the sleeping Campbell clan and massacre them at the Battle of Inverlochy in 1644.*

James Graham, Marquis of Montrose, the brilliant leader of the Royalist Highlanders.

Archibald Campbell, Marquis of Argyll, was Montrose's greatest enemy.

Naseby and the king's defeat

Prince Rupert, Charles I's dashing cavalry general, with his pet poodle, 'Boy'.

Despite his setbacks, Charles was still optimistic of victory. The Battle of Naseby destroyed his hopes once and for all. On their way to link up with Montrose's Highland army, the Royalists found the New Model Army blocking their way. They were forced to fight.

The battle started well for the smaller Royalist army. Rupert's full-blooded charge drove a section of Roundhead cavalry off the field. In the centre, the Royalist infantry pressed back the raw recruits of the opposite side.

Oliver Cromwell's superbly-drilled 'Ironsides' swung the battle Parliament's way. They smashed part of the Royalist cavalry and attacked the exposed flank of the Royalist infantry, forcing them to surrender.

Charles, in command of the reserves, ordered a charge which might yet have won the day, but the Earl of Carnwath grabbed his reins and stopped him, yelling, 'Will you go to your death?' The chance was lost. The king galloped away from the battlefield with only a few of his cavalry left.

Charles I dithers at a vital stage of the disastrous battle of Naseby in 1645.

In the next few months, the dwindling forces that remained loyal to Charles were defeated at the seige of Bristol and at the Battles of Langport and Stow-on-the-Wold. What could Charles do next? He could surrender to Parliament; abdicate and let his son become king; or give himself up to the Scots. He chose the latter.

On 27th April 1646, Charles left Oxford disguised as a servant, his long curls trimmed and his face covered by a false beard. The dangerous journey lasted a week until he reached the Scottish camp at Southwell, near Nottingham. Charles was kept prisoner there until, after eight months of stubbornly refusing to agree to the Scottish brand of Protestantism, the Scots 'sold' him to Parliament on 30th January 1647, exactly two years to the day before he was executed.

A group of Leveller soldiers meet to discuss how they want the country to be governed.

5 PARLIAMENT VERSUS THE ARMY

The Levellers

After the Battle of Stow-on-the-Wold, Sir Jacob Astley, a Royalist veteran, warned his enemies, 'you have done your work and may go play, unless you fall out among yourselves.' This is precisely what happened.

A serious rift appeared between the army and Parliament over the payment of the soldiers and what should be done with the king. Parliament, led by Denzil Holles, had almost reached a separate agreement with Charles and tried to disband the army, knowing that they would not support the pact with the king.

The army's reaction was swift and decisive. They assembled at Newmarket and ordered Cornet Joyce and 500 troopers to 'steal' the king from Holmby House where he was being held by parliamentary forces. They then invaded London and occupied Westminster. The army now held all the cards for deciding the future of the shattered country.

Unfortunately, a split developed in the army too, between the high-ranking officers and the ordinary soldiers, inspired by the radical ideas of 'free-born' John Lilburne and the 'Levellers'. The difference between the two sides became clear at a meeting of the army called the Putney Debates, when the Levellers put forward their ideas. As their name suggests, they wanted to level society and make it more equal. They hoped to abolish the monarchy and to allow all adults in the country, rich and poor alike, to elect a Parliament every two years. Today this sounds reasonable but in those days it was revolutionary.

In 1647 and 1649, soldiers, who sympathized with the democratic ideals of the Levellers, mutinied. Both times they were ruthlessly crushed. All the ringleaders, except Lilburne who was acquitted, were shot on Cromwell's orders. Levellerism, a political movement ahead of its time, ceased to exist.

John Lilburne, leader of the Levellers.

In 1649, the ringleaders of a Leveller mutiny are shot.

The Second Civil War and the 'Rump'

Charles tried to use the differences among his enemies to his own advantage. While pretending to negotiate with Cromwell and the other army leaders, he made a secret bargain with the Scots and waited for a Royalist uprising to free him and restore him to power. On 11th November 1647, he escaped to Carisbrooke Castle on the Isle of Wight, but found that he was no freer there than he had been as a prisoner of the army at Hampton Court.

Despite attempts to escape, Charles remained imprisoned throughout the second Civil War that was fought on his behalf from April to August 1648. From the Royalist point-of-view, it was a dismal and half-hearted affair. Royalist risings in Kent, Essex, and South Wales were crushed by the superior New Model Army. The Scots army invaded North England, this time in support of the king. They were routed at the Battle of Preston by Cromwell who chased them back over the border. It was over almost before it had begun.

There still remained the problem of what to do with

Charles I is imprisoned in Carisbrooke Castle on the Isle of Wight during the Second Civil War in 1648.

Charles I attempts to escape from imprisonment.

Charles. Many M.P.s were desperate to make peace with the king. They made secret negotiations with him behind the army's back. They also refused to agree with the army that Charles should be brought to justice for treason.

Cromwell was furious. For the second time, the army occupied London. On 5th December 1648, Colonel Pride and a band of heavily-armed soldiers surrounded the Parliament building and admitted only fifty hardline M.P.s who were known to support the army. The rest were barred from entering. A month later, this 'Rump' Parliament agreed to put Charles on trial for treason. Charles, knowing that his days were numbered, resigned himself to what lay before him.

6 THE REPUBLIC

The death of the king

30th January 1649, the day of the king's execution, was a raw and frosty winter's day. To keep warm, Charles asked to wear two shirts. He was worried that the biting cold might make him shiver. He did not want the watching crowds to think that he was frightened. Up to the last moment, Charles acted with great courage and dignity.

At his trial during the previous days, it was his judges who were nervous and frightened. One even wore a bullet-proof lining to his hat. Charles had called his own trial a sham. And so it was. Those who accused him had already decided he must die. Nothing anyone said in court could have altered that brutal fact. He was blamed for the bloodshed during the long and terrible years of Civil War, and condemned to lose his own life as a punishment. But only 59 out of the original 135 judges dared to sign his death warrant. Oliver Cromwell's signature appears third on that fateful document.

Charles 1's death warrant.

Normally, public executions were noisy and popular occasions. But this was very different. As Charles was brought on to the scaffold, the crowd fell silent. Even so, few could hear his defiant last words. There were too many 'Ironsides' between them and the platform. Charles said his last prayers and knelt to lay his head on the block. With a flicker of razor-sharp metal, the axe fell. A terrible groan went up from the crowd. Their king had been killed. Even those who had fought against him trembled at the consequences of the bloody act. During his life, Charles had failed to win the widespread sympathy of his people: by his death he achieved it.

Charles I prepares to go to his death on 30th January 1649.

Irish and Scottish rebellions

The king was dead. England was now a republic — a country without a king. The government was shared by the 'Rump' Parliament and a Council of State, led by Cromwell. Although the king, 'that man of blood', was no more, the bloodshed did not stop.

In 1641, the Catholics in the north of Ireland had slaughtered thousands of Protestants. In 1649, they remained violently opposed to the new government in England. Cromwell crossed the Irish Sea with a force of crack troops. He carried out his orders, which were to break and subdue the opposition, with ruthless efficiency.

Cromwell laid waste to the countryside and destroyed the cities of Drogheda and Wexford, massacring their

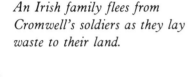

An Irish family flees from Cromwell's soldiers as they lay waste to their land.

citizens in cold blood. Cromwell's reputation has been severely dented by these acts of cruelty. It is little consolation to know that he thought at the time that it was, 'the righteous judgement of God upon those barbarous wretches.'

Cromwell returned from Ireland in May 1650, his task completed. A month later he was fighting a rebellion in Scotland, where the Scots had declared the dead king's son, Charles, the rightful heir. Using clever tactics, Cromwell defeated a larger Scottish army at the Battle of Dunbar on 3rd September 1650.

The Great Seal of the Commonwealth.

The Scots did not give up. They invaded England and reached as far south as Worcester where they were beaten once and for all, exactly a year after Dunbar. Charles hid up an oak tree, and only just escaped to France.

These rebellions made life difficult for the 'Rump' Parliament. The M.P.s argued among themselves, made mistakes, and got on the wrong side of the army. Cromwell grew tired of them. In an act more illegal than anything that Charles had ever done, he dismissed them by force on 20th April 1653.

7 THE SEARCH FOR A SETTLEMENT

The Protectorate

The Great Seal used during the English Protectorate.

Although the fighting had stopped, the country was deeply divided. It was like a boat rocking on a stormy sea, threatening to capsize at any moment. Cromwell realized that one man was needed at the helm.

On 16th December 1653, he accepted the offer to become Lord Protector of England. This made him the most important man in the republic. Some people even wanted to make him king, but he refused the crown because he would have made enemies of his old comrades in the New Model Army. He knew that without their support, he was nothing. Besides, how could a king-killer become king himself?

Cromwell used his new position as Lord Protector to act like a 'constable set to keep order in the parish'. He had lived through frightening times and wanted to restore law and order to the country. He also had to be constantly on guard against Royalist uprisings.

Cromwell had some success in stilling the raging waves during his five years in supreme control. Nevertheless, his conservatism disappointed many people and they became his bitter enemies. Some army officers had sworn to kill him if he accepted the offer of the throne. He walked in fear of his life and was always surrounded by an armed bodyguard.

In 1655, to protect himself and keep the country stable, Cromwell divided the nation into eleven districts. At the head of each he placed a major-general, loyal to himself, who had to keep order. These major-generals were hated as interfering busybodies, especially when they kept closing down inns! Indeed, the English hatred of military government stems from this time.

The task of uniting the English people wore down Cromwell's health. He became ill in 1658, and died on 3rd September, the same date as two of his greatest military victories.

Cromwell as Lord Protector discovers that governing England is not an easy task.

Charles II rides in triumph through the streets of London after his restoration to the throne of England in 1660.

The Restoration

After Oliver's death, Richard Cromwell, his eldest surviving son, became Lord Protector. He was totally unsuited for the job and preferred to spend his time hunting. Unlike his father, he did not command the respect and loyalty of the army. The leading generals — Fleetwood and Lambert — forced him to resign. Once again there followed a struggle for control between the army and Parliament.

The country was without a real leader and slipped quickly towards chaos. People panicked and searched around for someone who would make them feel safe once again. Now that Cromwell had gone, there seemed to be only one answer — Charles, son of Charles I.

Charles had spent years in exile, wandering around the countries of Europe, occasionally trying to re-kindle the fires of royalism in England. It had been a time of misery and discomfort. In late 1659, much to his surprise, he was invited by General Monk — who had been in charge of the army north of the Scottish border — to return to his homeland as king. To Monk, and others, there seemed no other way to return the country to sanity and stability.

Most people were overjoyed, but not everyone. A staunch republican swore that he would cut up the king into tiny pieces the size of herbs! Nevertheless, when Charles landed in England on 25th May 1660, he was given a rapturous welcome. As the dark, handsome man made his way up to London, his path was strewn with flowers, bells peeled, cannons fired, people cheered and the fountains ran with wine. There were similar scenes at his coronation. England, after a gap of eleven years, was governed once more by a king. The republic, like its founder Oliver Cromwell, was dead.

General George Monk, 1st Duke of Albemarle.

In one of the rare moments of fun during Charles II's long exile abroad, he dances with his sister at the Dutch court.

41

8 THE EFFECTS OF WAR

The fighting

Most people in England did not care which side won the war so long as they could live in peace and quiet. Many chose to ignore the fighting. In remote parts of the country, out of the way of the marauding armies, life went on much as before. As one priest said, 'I lived well because I laid low.'

In other parts of the country where it was impossible to escape the effects of war, people were not so lucky. Most families had a father, uncle or brother who was away from home fighting. Most knew the tragedy of a relative killed in battle.

The biggest disaster that could befall a village or town

A group of 'Clubmen' who hated the soldiers of both sides, barricade their village.

was to be in the path of an army. The villagers had to give 'free quarter' to the troops. This meant the soldiers would stay in their houses, eat their food and slaughter their animals. Worst still was to be in the way of a poorly-paid and ill-disciplined army on one of its drunken rampages through the countryside, pillaging and looting.

People grew to hate the sight of soldiers, whether they were Roundheads or Cavaliers. They became sick of war, tired of the heavy taxes and the disruption of their lives. Groups of local people banded together who did not care who governed them — king or Parliament — so long as they could lead normal lives.

These 'Clubmen' armed themselves with scythes and pitchforks and fought off whichever side threatened the security of their own little community. They wanted only peace in their own land. By 1660, the best hope for peace was the restoration of Charles II, which explains why he was welcomed back, even by those who had fought against him and his father.

A typical countryman at the time of the Civil War.

Religion

Today, religion is unimportant to many people. In those days, it was everything. Everyone believed in God and thought that their lives were guided by Him. They lived rough and harsh lives so the promise of a happy life-after-death, if you kept in God's good books, must have been very appealing.

The events of the Reformation had thrown everything into the melting-pot. During the Civil War, religious

A Puritan tells off his children for picking berries at Christmas time.

groups flourished which had different ideas about what the Bible said and how they should worship. They came under various banners, calling themselves Ranters, Baptists, Fifth Monarchists, or Quakers. During this time, they had great freedom. For a few months in 1653, a new Parliament met. It was called the 'Barebones' Parliament after one of its members, Praise-God Barebones. It gave these groups a brief taste of power.

Cromwell was tolerant of these groups until they stepped out of line, when he could be very harsh. James Naylor, one of the Quaker leaders, made a Christ-like entry into Bristol on a donkey. For the cheek of pretending to be Jesus, he was whipped and pilloried.

For Puritans, religion was a serious business and because life and religion were like inseparable twins, life itself was a serious matter. They had strict life-styles and could be real kill-joys. Even their names — 'Kill-sin Pimple', for example — suggest a lack of gaiety.

Any rich ceremony or lavish entertainment was frowned upon, especially if it was carried out on Sunday — the Lord's Day. They even did away with the festivities of Christmas, and children were punished if they were caught picking berries for decorations. It cannot have been much fun growing up in a Puritan household, with so many rules and regulations.

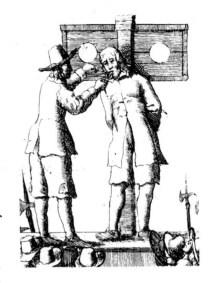

The Quaker, James Naylor, is punished in the pillory for pretending to be Christ.

A Puritan man and his wife in the 1640's.

Town life

During the war, most towns were turned into fortresses to protect them from attack. In London, by far the largest English town with a population of 400,000, ditches were dug and streets bricked up to keep the Royalists out. In other parts of the country, towns like Bristol were regularly beseiged and changed hands several times.

Life was tough for the townspeople in the war. Their towns were turned into military garrisons. There were heavy taxes and food shortages. It was hard to sleep at night with the place full of drunken and looting soldiers.

A few people grew rich from the war but, for the most part, it had a disastrous effect on the trade which was carried out in towns. Business could not go on as normal. Ships lay idle in the docks, cargoes rotted, warehouses stood empty. Merchants wrung their hands in despair as their wealth slipped away from them.

When the fighting stopped and Cromwell became Lord Protector, trade picked up and law and order returned to England's towns. Puritan magistrates were cruelly harsh with any convict, however small his crime. Although it was safer to walk the streets with the Puritans in control, they could do little to make those streets cleaner and free from disease.

Plague was a constant threat in towns. There was no town planning in those days. Houses were built close together and crammed full of people. The streets stank of decaying rubbish. There was no running water. In the insanitary conditions, disease travelled fast and struck rich and poor alike. This was especially true in time of war. Towns were grim places to live in, and yet they were growing all the time because they were centres of fashion and entertainment for the rich, and held the tantalizing promise of interesting work for the poor.

A London merchant.

A lady wearing the plain clothes fashionable at the time.

A merchant looks unhappy as his ship lies idle in the docks.

Country life

The population of England was a mere five million in the seventeenth century. A large percentage lived and worked in the country and almost everybody worked in agriculture. Most of the land belonged to a few rich landowners who lived in sumptuous country mansions. The other country folk were small farmers who rented land from the lord of the manor, and farm labourers who lived in one-roomed hovels and worked for the farm owner for a tiny wage.

The war had a serious impact on all these people. The rich were forced to pay huge sums of money to whichever side knocked on their door first. Their houses were often stripped bare by bands of pillaging soldiers.

The poorer people worked from dawn to dusk, scratching together a living. If they were fortunate, they might own a small vegetable patch or a few animals. Occasionally they looked up from their work and saw soldiers and horsemen clattering down the country lanes in search of

food for the armies. They had no protection from these rampaging troops and would be forced to surrender whatever supplies were demanded of them.

There were some people who had no land, no home, and no job. They became vagrants, wandering from place to place in search of employment. The war at least gave them the chance of becoming soldiers, which was better than nothing.

However, for most of these country people, the war was an unwelcome nuisance. Their loyalties were towards their own community and village. Men, women and children wanted to be left alone in peace to work in the fields, spin yarn for cloth, or work as milkmaids or grooms in a country mansion. So long as this happened, it did not matter who governed the country. Life was harsh but simple, and they hated anyone who meddled with their affairs.

A typical country scene in the 17th century. In the foreground, a woman spins yarn. Behind her, a gentleman hunts deer.

Family life

The war had a terrible effect on family life. Fathers and sons were forced to leave the comfort of their homes for the dangers of the battlefield. Many never returned. Wives were abandoned to care for the children and protect their houses as best they could. Some, like the wife of the Earl of Derby in Lathom House, bravely defended their houses against siege. War and bad harvests made life especially hard for the poorer people whose lives were an uphill struggle to feed their families.

After the war, family life slowly returned to normal. It remained hard and uncomfortable for the poorer people, and more civilized for the better-off. Each family had its daily routine. In Puritan households this pattern was often interrupted by sessions of prayer. The family gathered together, bowed their heads, and asked God for his protection and help. These Puritan families dressed plainly, ate sparingly and furnished their houses simply.

Puritans often met during the day to say their prayers and listen to Bible readings.

Not everyone was a Puritan, and family life for those who were not was a more relaxed and lively affair. Life in the great country houses bustled with activity. The lady of the house controlled many servants to help her to care for her family. There were laundry maids to make sure that her family's clothes were smart and clean, servants to wait at table and gardeners to grow the herbs she used as medicine to keep her children healthy.

The family came together for meals which they ate without forks. The men wore their hats at table. We would probably be horrified by their manners! We would also be shocked by how seldom they washed, and how they had to go outside to the lavatory because there were no inside toilets. In those days, family life was far more primitive than we know it today.

A Puritan family in their simply furnished home.

Amusements

Recreation was more simple and straightforward at this time. Children could enjoy themselves with games of skittles, playing on the swings or walking on stilts. Adults had different forms of enjoyment, depending on their incomes. The rich spend their free time hunting, hawking, horse-racing and fencing. The less well-off either sat drinking in smoky taverns playing cards, risked their necks in a murderous version of football, or watched the bloodthirsty sports of bear-baiting and cockfighting. In severe winters, Londoners enjoyed frost fairs on the frozen waters of the River Thames.

While the Puritans were in control, most of these activities were banned. The stern-minded Puritans believed that they encouraged ungodly behaviour and wickedness, and had to be stopped.

Cromwell closed the theatres. Maypoles were chopped down and morris dancing was forbidden. There were to

Life became more pleasant after the Restoration in 1660. Here are some of the popular games people played.

52

be no celebrations at Christmas, which was now to be spent saying sorry to God for having had such a good time in the past! On Sundays it was almost impossible to move without being punished. One woman was put in the stocks for mending a dress on the Lord's Day. Others were fined for drinking or for singing.

For most people, Sunday was the only day that they did not work, so they were very unhappy at not being able to relax and enjoy themselves as they wished. It is certain that people continued to play games and took the risk of being caught, even some of those who called themselves Puritans.

At the Restoration, these bans were lifted. Charles II reintroduced the old sports and entertainments. It was no longer a sin to play music, to dance or to watch plays. Life became more light-hearted. The Puritans had won the Civil War, but failed to win the hearts of the people.

CAROLVS·I·D:G·MAG·BRITANN·FRAN·ET·HIB·REX

9 SUMMING UP THE AGE

The story of Oliver Cromwell and the Civil War is an extraordinary one. It covers a period when strong feelings about religion and politics led to violence and bloodshed. It was a time of heroism and despair, of intrigue and adventure. For years, family life was interrupted, and there were only a few who escaped the horrors of war.

War happened because of a breakdown in the relationship between a king and his people, as represented in Parliament. Both came to hold different views about how the country should be governed. The two sides drifted apart and soon found that they had no common ground. Their deep distrust for one another led to a struggle which could only have one winner.

After many fierce battles and the loss of 100,000 lives, the king was beaten and, in one of the most shocking events in English history, was executed. England was so used to being governed by one person that chaos followed Charles I's death. Oliver Cromwell stepped into the breach. For five years he was king in all but name.

Cromwell had an almost impossible task of trying to unite a country that was still deeply divided. As Lord Protector he combined firmness with tolerance to achieve a remarkable stability. When he was in power, England came to be feared and respected by the other European nations.

When Cromwell died, the cement which had held the republic together, crumbled. In 1660, Charles II was restored to the throne as the man most likely to soothe the differences that divided the country. But this turbulent period did achieve some lasting results. Never again would a king be able to rule without Parliament for eleven years; the ideas of the Levellers are accepted by most democratic countries today; and the freedom to worship God in one's own way was soon to be achieved.

Left *Oliver Cromwell and Charles I, the leaders of the two sides in the Civil War, and the Houses of Parliament.*

Table of dates

1599 Oliver Cromwell is born.

1603 James I becomes King of England.

1620 Oliver Cromwell marries Elizabeth Bourchier.

1625 King James I dies. Charles I becomes King of England and Scotland.

1625-29 War against Spain.

1628 Petition of Right.
Failure of Buckingham's expedition to La Rochelle.
Buckingham is assassinated by John Felton.

1629-40 Charles I's eleven years of personal rule without Parliament.

1636 John Hampden is tried in court for refusing to pay 'Ship Money'.

1637 Three well-known Puritans are publicly mutilated.

1639-40 Bishops' wars between England and Scotland.

1640 Start of the Long Parliament.

1641 Strafford's execution.

1642 Charles I attempts to arrest the five Members of Parliament.
Charles I raises his standard at Nottingham. Civil War starts.
Battle of Edgehill.

1644 Battle of Marston Moor.
Battle of Tippermuir — Montrose's victory in Scotland.

1645 New Model Army is formed.
Battle of Naseby.
Battle of Philiphaugh — Montrose is defeated.
Archbishop Laud is executed.

1646 Scots 'sell' Charles I to the English Parliament.

1648 Second Civil War (April-August).
Colonel Pride purges Parliament.

1649 Trial and execution of Charles I.
Cromwell invades Ireland and sacks Drogheda and Wexford.
Leveller mutiny is crushed and the ringleaders shot.

1650 Montrose is executed.
Battle of Dunbar. Scots and Charles II are defeated.

1651 Charles II and the Scots are defeated at Battle of Worcester.

1653 Oliver Cromwell expels the 'Rump' Parliament.
'Barebones' Parliament sits for a short while.
Oliver Cromwell is appointed Lord Protector.

1655-57 Cromwell divides England into 11 military districts which are ruled by major-generals.

1657 Oliver Cromwell refuses the title of king.

1658 Oliver Cromwell dies.
Richard Cromwell becomes Lord Protector.

1660 Charles II is restored to the throne of England.

New words

Abdicate   When a king or queen chooses to give up his/her crown in favour of someone else.

Catholic   The religion which claims to be the one true Church of God. The pope, who lives in Rome, is the head of the Catholic Church.

Civil War   A war fought between people who live in the same country.

Commonwealth   A label given to the years 1649-1660 when England was not governed by a king but by a government supposedly interested in the welfare of all British people.

Conscripts   Persons who are forced to join and serve in an army.

Council of State   A group of important men who helped the Lord Protector run the country.

Court   The group of people who surrounded the king wherever he was staying.

Democracy   A form of government where everyone has a say in how their country should be run.

Fens   Flat, marshy land in East Anglia.

Hovel   A very poor dwelling-place.

Ironsides   Cromwell's highly-disciplined cavalry troopers.

Lord Protector   The title given to Oliver Cromwell in 1653 as the most important man in the country.

Magistrate   A man in the law courts who has the power to punish people if they are found guilty of committing a crime.

M.P. (Member of Parliament)   A man who voices the wishes of his local community in Parliament.

Musket   A long-barrelled gun.

New Model Army   The name given to the reorganized Roundhead army in 1645.

Parliament   An assembly of the most important and wealthy people who met at Westminster to help the king run the country. Then, as now, it was divided into two parts, the House of Lords and the House of Commons.

Pike   A long wooden pole with a sharp iron point, like a long spear.

Protestant   A religious group that grew up after the Reformation. It 'protested' at some of the preachings of the pope and the Catholic Church.

Puritans   A group of serious-minded people who were very religious. They wanted to purify the Church of any remaining Catholic ideas. There were many Puritans in England at this time.

Reformation   A European religious movement in the sixteenth century that changed the things that the reformers thought were wrong with the Catholic Church, and started the Reformed, or Protestant, churches.

Republic   A form of government without a king or a queen.

Restoration   In 1660, Charles II was 'restored' to the throne which was rightfully his since his father's death in 1649.

Ship money   A tax that used to be imposed on coastal towns only. Charles I caused a rumpus by raising it throughout the country.

Toleration   When a person who is in the position of making laws allows people to hold their own beliefs, even though he might disagree with them.

Treason   The crime of betraying your country.

Further information

Places to visit

Museums Every county in Britain has dozens of museums open to the public, far too many to list here. Certain London museums hold collections of artefacts from this period — the Museum of London, the Geffrye Museum, the National Army Museum, the Victoria and Albert Museum, and the Tower of London are all worth a visit.

Famous sites Many towns in England were affected by the Civil War in some way. It is interesting to discover what happened in your own local area during the war — which side it supported and whether there were any battles fought nearby. If you want to see the shirt that Charles I wore at his execution, visit Longleat; or make a trip to the Isle of Wight to see where Charles I was imprisoned in Carisbrooke Castle. A visit to Berkeley Castle in Gloucestershire is fun too because you can see the damage done to the building by Cromwell's artillery. It is worth writing to the National Trust enclosing a stamped, addressed envelope. They should be able to tell you more about the places to visit nearer to your home.

Libraries The local library can always give information about the best places to visit, both near your home and farther afield. Most libraries have a section on local history. Try to discover what was going on in your area during the Civil War and the Protectorate.

Books

Barnaby, James, *Puritan and Cavalier — the English Civil War* (Gollancz 1977)

Cowie, Leonard, *Trial and Execution of Charles I* (Wayland 1972)

Clarke, Amanda, *Growing up in Puritan Times* (Batsford)

Crockatt, John, *The Battle of Marston Moor* (Lutterworth 1976)

Liversidge, Douglas, *The Restoration* (Wayland 1977)

Peach, L. Du Garde, *Oliver Cromwell* (Ladybird 1963)

Purves, Amanda, *Oliver Cromwell* (Wayland 1977)

Index

Picture Acknowledgements

The illustrations in this book were supplied by: courtesy of the Trustees of the British Museum 17 (top);
John R. Freeman (Photographers) and Co. Ltd. 43; Mansell Collection 11, 27 (bottom), 34; National
Portrait Gallery 4, 17 (bottom), 41 (top); Queen's Collection (Lord Chamberlain's Office) 41 (bottom).
The remaining photographs are from the Wayland Picture Library.